BURIED AT SEA

First published 2006 by
Worple Press
PO Box 328
Tonbridge
Kent TN9 1WR

British Library Cataloguing in Publication data.
A catalogue record for this book is available from the British Library

ISBN 1-905208-06-5
ISBN 13: 9781905208067

Worple Press is an independent publisher specialising in poetry, art
and alternative titles. **Worple Press** can be contacted at:

Worple Press
PO Box 328
Tonbridge
Kent TN9 1WR

Tel: 01732 368958
E-mail: theworpleco@aol.com

Worple Press gratefully acknowledges Arts Council support

Typeset and printed at Peepal Tree Press

Iain Sinclair

BURIED AT SEA

worple
press

CONTENTS

Trailer   11

MARINADE

The Argument   16
Yesterday's Money   17
Eden Roc Stars   18
Body Tourism   19
Mouse Semen Milked   20
Currently Dead (Indians)   21
Ascent   22
The Beach   22
Owl Towel   23
Sleeping-Off Insomnia   24
Treading Fruit   25
Ink   25
The Back of His Face   26
Torque Radio   27
Lies Like Lies   28
Dumb Oracle   29
Aryan Dates   30
Language Dentistry   31
Permission to Crenellate   32
Über Drei   33
Promise Everything, Sign Nothing   34
The Influencing Machine   35
Fetch   36
Aftermath   38

BLAIR'S GRAVE

Blair's Grave   41
Aftermath   54

PATRICK HAMILTON

Patrick Hamilton in St. Leonards on Sea   58
Aftermath   65

THE OPENING OF THE FIFTH SEAL:
WALTER SICKERT, ALEISTER CROWLEY
& THE CHAPMAN BROTHERS

Buried at Sea   69
Double Exposure   70
Standing Man in Spectacles, Lecturing Seated Woman   72
Meat Raffle   72
Keiller's Dundee   73
Night Visitor   74
Fishy Oils   75
Maybe Oregon   76
Moderato Cantabile   77
Money Mystics   78
Broken Hat   78
Sickert at Dieppe   79
Castled   81
Hastings Opera   82
Volaverunt   83
26 August 1875   84
Post-Office   84
Channel Hopping   85
Platz Angst   88
Disasters of War   89
8 Knots   90
9 October 2005   91
Aftermath   92

Acknowledgements   95
Select Viewing   96

BURIED AT SEA

SHOOTING-
SCRIPT
CONFESSIONAL

TRAILER

Hastings every day was filling...
A morning's reading by the ocean's rim
> Thomas Hood

Hastings
 is the lower jaw of an alligator
> Ed Dorn

'You a praying man?' he said.
'Uh-huh.'
'Good, gonna have to be when the Chinese take over.'
> Bob Dylan

MARINADE

15

Lounging on a high shelf above a busy coast road, the poet acknowledges the sound of the sea, while remaining ordinarily insensitive to the transit of marine light: cloud formations, wave rhetoric, tricks of sunrise and sunset. Nervously, he attempts snapshots from the balcony. Newsprint. Ink stains on wrinkled hands. Flickering gas. A mash of crab claws, onions, black pepper, gunpowder. Condensation. He dates each entry in the blue notebook; strokes the fake parrot, remembering the empty cage in a Welsh garage. His first grandfather fading, quietly, into grey.

YESTERDAY'S MONEY

'private runways to the Truth'
Manny Farber

Who cleans the crease blacks Kazan's shoes
skin curtains, reflections of lamplight
Chelsea Hotel telephone-corridor rings
dead Steinbeck, dotty electronic flash
two succoured troubled men in edge-time
freshwhite shirts open at the neck,
bone-button, free radical, downcast eyes
play camera innocent, one filthy pipe
desert-punished Marxists, cordial news
barbiturate chicken breast, rank
chlorine, can you love
a stalled American dreamscape?
River Jews in celebrity hothouse,
concerned about carpets, London labels
Political detectives launder bloody sheets
virus passed before midnight strikes
shallow drawer lined with crappy sand

What's out there we assume is blue
butter pressed by serrated blade
into landscape format, salty-fresh
old affections dress balcony waif
female mammal nude, fur heels
above necklace of isometric light
honeysuckle Corniche, doctored
stitch: Scott & Zelda, pain-sob
mopped by warm linen, proper
coffee assault, arm around
one mass of wet together
What's in the prints today?
cold cream under eye, his vas
ectomy removed womb, flush
periods instead of facile adjectives
waltz schmaltz, liquid gold
drooping cypress, rocks of the bay
Resting writer's snaggle teeth, top
of the range Merc leased by torture boss
Russian oil in airport shock, double
sparkle quinine mineral water please

BODY TOURISM

'It's unimaginable. It'll come'
Anita Brookner

News of this season's war comes over the horizon
without a ripple, blank as paperpulp
scorched hair, pork & petrol, hot black
spiral columns of harm:
2 cars broadside on desert highway, we salute
video tremor (undead with platinum credit),
it takes quality sound to ruin such a morning,
shingle scraped, Dutch wreckage
The poet in his current (too current) self-disguise
justifies the hole in the page
holds his spectacles in a very peculiar way
meat-gloves, old old
as he is, eyeless, freaked for random
acquaintance, blinking
journeyman up from Smoke,
odd combo, diamond sweatshirt and rather
slick (sharky) jacket, sentimental bite:
surrealist tearaway now elder statesman (extant)

Let in, sea doesn't care, the poet
he hears gulls sneeze through glass

MOUSE SEMEN MILKED

'A little rubbing up, croup to flies'
Catherine Millet

It happens, the wormwood & the retro
spective regret
fame-train, gravy: how bored can
boredom filters get? Kiddy-grope doorway
amplified by naked flicker-bulb
It's strange nothing has changed
beyond a certain dignity of sideburn, he
laughs: 'name?' Sorry can't recall
man who says he knew a doctor once
woman wallowing in fat
artlessly defamed on dirty bed,
piss artist run out of piss & syringes
Dry sick, rushed lunch, retch vest
shaved Parmesan the cheesiest
of your formal snaps, death's pimp
head in hands, last coach for Brighton

CURRENTLY DEAD (INDIANS)

naked meat inside chocolate
rabbit-fish
skinned sea
walking the only way
not to leave your soul (*your* soul)
behind, proper stride
length of iron ladder, out-tide
recorded Bulverhythe wreck
mast (stone) deck (rim)
portrait of the week: Ghost of a Flea

cliffs crumble like Scottish teeth
bits of Spitfire brought ashore
cigarette card, suitable gift
for Father's Day, pasted grid across
mall table, lit by plant decay
absence of monkeys
Vigour of my Youth & Genius
under oppression
'are you – who you – are'
withdrawn whitewoman
cherries on dress, grey
hair, more & less what I deserve

ASCENT

scene of the crime gloves
fingers bent
nosegay of pink
(white too)
high narrow steps in wet-light
official view, knife in the back

THE BEACH

stripping to coarse hemp
rutting to knot
(quiet) yachts circle small bay
'it's a lot of things,' she said
'but it's not poetry'

undercarriage dangling
diamond pattern on sand floor

OWL TOWEL

'Ashy light in which at that time he lived'
Joseph Conrad

Mackerel memories, bright shoal
boneless heart-in-pillow
soft cell, carried to ocean's edge,
one eye to heaven
I hang in wave, bottled
without border, thermometer
like pen, practice
against fact of sinking, flux
burns with city weight, voice
accidental, remedial
a holiday, cut feet on pebble shelf
taste untasted, old-new
baby, heavy with implication
infected by germoline mother
how kind
shadows little huts
eleven fish lifted from beach
that first night, garlic & fennel
a dash of wax: cut wrist, warm silt sea

SLEEPING-OFF INSOMNIA

'all the gang a bigger haycock make'
John Clare

There are alloys of absence
celluloid selves
other-us, everpresent
in the not-actual crease
between water & land
How they make it, lacking
perfect recall, film-scratch
they bleed, hot
honeybreath, waspish
discovered versions of
who, of, walkingseeing
remembering, birth-house
white tile, open gown,
lean smooth legs
sudden at field edge
regular, what
are we, before the
story begins, copper beech
out from your window
into my ear my heart
the holy living of
those who managed it, once

TREADING FRUIT

territory 'as described'
& territory in which she stands
hungry for shoes

INK

among those washed ashore
on the morning of 28 November 2003
a rectangular box of frozen CALAMARES
from Monterey, California
blue as One-Eyed Jacks Pacific
empty as the dollar eyes of Marlon Brando

THE BACK OF HIS FACE

Cutting miscutting photo-border
upturned collar smoke, the action
of her act: 21 grams
weight of a human soul
lost at death, which dog weighs meat
waits on the waiter, in film-time
beside wet road, naked dancer
in oily leather coat is watched
the instant of it, her loss
riverside, by hundreds later millions
as print thins words vanish
true weight of soul unredeemed
on soap-factory railtrack

TORQUE RADIO

'the sea, the sea fills the whole horizon'
Tom Raworth

talk of foxes, flatheads & tyre-ironed
torsos left at verge of hot roads south,
the maggot mask the un
boned hank of shoulderwrap,
Hollywood's freckled skincream,
sell me something: a water cannon,
memory of scarlet hunt the slipper sniffing
mutton-shock of Charlotte R's pubic ridge
slabnaked for chlorine poolman's
gallic tact: grave plot suppressed,
wire-kisses, that's evidence that's payback

since I slept on hops, crunchywheat pillow
stinking of river, my nights have
new words: 'circumlocution'
elocution's dumb cousin, torched car in woods
nature's barbed wire
drowsy sow dreams of A21, the swollen
balls of a sated boar, his corrugated
shack, zeppelin prick never
got off ground, the absent landlord
who clips peacocks' wings
deserves his imprisoned wife's pointy
ears, fairy story without fairies
in default of necessary marine proofs

Like a land mermaid, her
empty leather suit-
case, brass corners &
fat with air, full mouth
eager to swallow
ETERIA smoke
Heels screw, cut low
to brand infamous sway,
nicotine trenchcoat
rancid butter hair, the
cowboy had to wear
3 undershirts to pad
his muscle contract,
it's what happens when
the middle goes missing
      Suicide tent
perched in high desert
gambling horses
            unbroken
celluloid noise-crews,
not leaving Las Vegas

ARYAN DATES

'I had led a reclusive, melancholy life and been ill-married.'
W.G. Sebald

across England leaves burn red, umbrellas
sea-winters, left alone, colour holiday elsewhere
those hands, fingers splayed, postcard
floats over Beachy Head, plastic water bottle
resolved unresolved
'adrift in the human breeze'
his voice, one-third replete
hard swallow, rock-rain, loose coat
fixed in hat box
when that double rainbow happened
I'd run out of film (again)(again)
you'll have to take my word for it

boiled milk & batteries
wrapped in wet newspaper
– a hat?
choke of font on bumpy tongue
spell: oil moustache, corset
of metallurgy (allergic to metal),
geopolitics, food, air
conditioned road or hard
mountain clag in shoe (no socks),
poulticed with icecream & cut
mushroom cornplasters, add saltpeter
fuse of kindness
radio-water:
segregated ablutions or dosh-curry

PERMISSION TO CRENELLATE

'a sequence of images is no evidence'
Tom Raworth

Give candle to the midwife who,
motherless childspawn, rocks in support stocking
in mortgaged beach hut. Opposite minister
has no pit, not called upon to oppose
to stand, yes, migrant in wallpaper dress
tented on green, grape-fed foxes:
no lecture lasts the first is
whips & wheels, English hedge for hire
second movement is the last story
runs out, we return,
foolish, scent words to
yellow envelope, kindness kills the
pyramid, blunt photos iterate
hurt: lordy, how spam-boss guzzles

ÜBER DREI

'I am more real in the winter'
Iris Murdoch

centric beatitude the sea concludes
benign refusal to commiserate or
scold-bridle or hide morning sun from
bronze foam on the old lunatic's
aboriginal teeth, Californian orthodontics
restore my ill-suited friend
a cake of emulsion on the gashouse door
slow collapse into zero:
the fringe, liquid, is pretty much left alone
until phone trills with performance news,
hysteric, leather bikini, misattributed
Templar rituals imported like mushy dates
Jersey carnation for the wedding
of a Bishopsgate gangster and a stuffed mule

    Let go, let it go, use grey
        salt heals mimed thrust, a paw
    another empty charity pew

PROMISE EVERYTHING, SIGN NOTHING

'The worst he did was wave his stick and shout at the sea'
(Memoir of Bram Stoker)

sea-photos,
no salt
heart on plate,
gold warmth of
soft-arm smell,
his father's wool ticks on slope
intimate barbering
accused of walking exclusively
with white males:
pink-soap dispenser,
keep one coin, silence
richer than sheep
strangers of 4-bloods step out from
drowned church

THE INFLUENCING MACHINE

'The form of the bone is really similar to that of an almond'
Thomas Love Beddoes

Twenty locks in basket, shaved
terror, clinker-ridge
folded urchin, orphan thought
'delusions of reference'
without egoic pivot, nail, closewoven
air loom, taste iron in steady
rain, Moorgate aflood
'cacodemonomania'
eruption, the sea
stands on its head, red sun
over floodplain, seen from motorway
solitude, improvised cell
portrait of discontinued poet
framed on wall
performance dying, Tibetan bells,
bloody stone shat on dish,
blink rapidly,
healthy indifference to present world

FETCH
for Andrew Kötting

'When your daddy was a little girl, we used to fetch him down here.' So fetch him now, whoever, wherever, which daddy. Identity migrates. Sympathetic contours, discriminations of memory. Lazy souls drift south: biscuit tins, newspaper cuttings, marine exile. Victorian estate-agents with Kodak cameras. Everything slides, out of clay, chalk, clear-flowing streams, watercress beds; into greensand, shingle. So fetch. Fetch him to a steep beach. Smooth, sharp stones. Letter to a dead man.

Spectral copies of photographs laid on a table. Little, it must be admitted, of the son; his films watched, in my own sitting-room, rather than their proper setting, the cinema. Evidence? Car with the number plate MU. 'Pop music's most esoteric creations: Zodiac Mindwarp and the Love Reaction and The Justified Ancients of Mu Mu.'

I declined to look into my own father's dead eyes, pre-incineration, preferring to remember him alive, moving. His face is often there now: re-coloured, Balkan. I impersonate the impersonation, false doctor. Clasped hands, angle of head. The choice will come around again: my son remembering his grandfather remembering me.

The De La Warr pavilion seems to be the right setting: deck chairs, brass band. 'We are about to embark on a journey.' Bexhill is where the stiffs come, at ease with themselves. Wardrobes in charity shops. The Purgatorio at the end of Jim Thompson's novel, *The Getaway*.

I set out early from Hackney, cellophane flowers grafted on concrete posts. The narrative of a life reduced to four images. The grave, inscrutable child. The father in proud blazer. The amused (terrified) citizen. The iconic corpse. I found water, followed it: Grand Union Canal, Thames (ferry to Hilton Hotel), Christopher Marlowe's memorial slab. 'Cut is the branch that might have grown full straight'. Held up just once: Prince Charles and motorcade visiting a newly heritaged sewage plant.

Walking won't do it, halt the image flow. Stills flick into an alien biography. Life happens, when it happens, in the narrow white columns between prints. Detective story. Field report. Love letter. Fable.

1. A boy's jacket.
2. Cars parked outside a European building.
3. A section of boat, misty jetty.
4. The cross. The coffin.

Already we know too much. White spirit explodes from aperture. Box-boat slides into ocean of flame. The man wakes, sits up, raises his arm. He screams. We seal our ears with wadded newspaper.

AFTERMATH

Photographs. Many are overexposed, light-blasted, with a faded quality beyond their age, suggesting things barely glimpsed despite the simple nature of the objects and the spare captions.

Don DeLillo

The poetic, posed as an absolute, is seen as that which exposes the utopian tendencies and blind alleys of the historical, but always comes up against its own limitations, its absence of foundation and legitimacy, and can only be accomplished in a fragmentary fashion, broken forms, fiction and reflection interwoven with humour.

Youssef Ishaghpour

His own bomb did not go off. He fled and was later found dead in the sea.

Independent on Sunday (24 July 2005)

BLAIR'S GRAVE

BLAIR'S GRAVE

'They had tongues like angels but cloven feet'
Oliver Cromwell

monkeyheaded earthenware drinking vessels
clatterrattle at behest of the man who blows
bad wind, fabricated facemask
unbuilds ziggurat of denial
talks piety, sweat-meniscus drying blue
'I want I want', no trust-
worthy rung on ladder, so shred it
believe what I say I say: foul-paper straw

II

your city will be underwater, fool
better so, intimate
sleeves rolled, wild eyes won't focus
everything swims, dirty glass
eyes for onions, software
coloured wire, bird substitutes
duck and swim through skin
you cough: words are broken plates

III

what would occur if the beard of Dr Griffiths
were appointed, asthmatic wheeze
master, workboss, retired labour
lord, in place of mendacity, warp-truth
headlamps 'like a patch of daylight'
by command, distressed
distressed bears huddle from
evangelists: anxious speculators on a melting shore

IV

hasty strings at eventide, question time
in Cherie orchard, cold finger's rectal probe
hedged fleece circumlocution
office offends dignity, he cannot
cut the mustard gas, cressbed on chalk
which prime minister delivered most sick
notes which fucked least, 'counter-
compositional thrusts' & cancelled kids

V

peppering belly with hurt food, waiting on
chequered cloth, entertainers named & shamed
ventriloquised paste, nothing to say becomes
nothing to do, roll under floodtide
stacked capital in drowned sheds,
mortars lobbed at mud fort
will they be burgled at the back door
with pokers & nuclear shingle, pilgrim
caste badge: poverty chic or obedience

VI

most of the food we receive is sacked Kurd
'English-Turkish-Greek-Continental'
grand alliance united nations redgreen
display tomatoes peppers dates brown
onions oranges with stalks lottery sales
to locally poor cancer ward horseflesh
afternoons funding exchange rate dis-
satisfied CCTV records: knife damage

VII

like a boatman up against the wall
seawall? pretty much so, grave blocks
of uneven size weight distribution, bareheaded
missing & unsure how to stand,
right fist curled childish other loose
in pocket, touches hair-flesh, beard on
wrong part of the head, turn it, the fire:
food, dance, the mystical, history, crime

VIII

summer barque studio storm
like fireflies the lantern'd boats far out
across the dark lake, oil rigs & prisons,
staggers ape-gait through
neon showers, 3 years slumbering on
the banks of the Ocean, died in LA
car crash theme: reshot, recut
fever, malaria, bicycle, vamp
he picked his chauffeurs for their looks

IX

anyplace but Utah hard snow the things you do
all the time are the ones to forget Perugino
madonna postcard lying on blue cloth of
Blake book, we were dreaming
the nuns the Bardot girl
do it again begin where we let
go, out of the box bursts
waterstorm to freeze the city's previously
unrevealed source: opium gum, stiff tongues

X

comb the beach for scotsmen who can't swim
to Malaya through the bottom of a bottle
fire alcove benches excited monologue
sights in yellow telescope are
blame not be apportioned
individual purchasers of ethical coffee or lords
of conspicuous charity stepping from full-
bellied aircraft in dark glasses which they remove
for interviews, much water still tastes of sewage

XI

Gordon Brown plants tree in Kenyan slum
we're not the Mail we could stretch to 600
in the Hotel North the monkey never dies
city of invisible rails no sky
chili dogs chase empty beer bottles
see you around Molly raincoat
neon spells bead the narrator is
dead: cinched belt a world without news

XII

clouds rack the judge's low ceiling
illusory flag-world of ghetto
archetypes, mammal miss her jack-nerved
dealer, tarot nativity sword
I know that old boy he used to be a boxer
when chafing cares shall cool at last
otherwise he must live out in misery
lamentable time, bet the house, bet fast

XIII

police ambulance air gunship
guilty of everything swastika armband
bad son manacles in the interpreter's house
spike threatens carotid artery moslem radio
bodies dance in hot air nothing gives
wrist slap tapioca tube mum's relief
family name friend saw old man rushing from
krugerrand bank with bags of hot loot
therefore he swet, and did quake for fear

XIV

if you can't force gates of death a blown safe
on the low-way to Beckton problematic pilgrimage
stalls in aftermath air inside burns
portal a mocking quotation labour caduceus
try the role you could not fulfil and now
father's kinder breath puffs a shopping bag
rats worms wires replace blood no virtual will
roof of strategic walk: alone and sneezing

XV

again trapped against seafret invited
to pelt the old gentleman with mud, self-generated
if practicable, by handful, gypsy
american clothing, soft on stiffening body
has known cold & cell, damage, eyes won't open
until there is something solid to view,
empty traffic invitation to shoot
never never allow this impropriety: reproduction

XVI

which wife slips open window other men know
unfixed framework dried stone
sponsor's message resolves fingerprint of god
painter of nocturnes, watercolours, glaze under
glaze, rectangle of river, one racing certainty
non-verifiable external witness & inward
prompting anxiety of influence, pulpy red
fibres, polyps, sand: it's there & you know it

XVII

BEWARE THE SEA. IT HAS THE SMELL OF BLOOD, OR LIFE
or letter set at paper-hanging angle, painter
bespectacled before wall of sea photos
sea-on-sea, & fear, paper will give way before
storm erupts, real water, overwhelming in dip &
crush IT FLOWS GENTLY THIS END if you
watch with eyes and let dogs swim in your place
I LIVE IN HOPE OF A BROADCAST he relents
coal clinker WILL NEVER EVER RETURN

XVIII

life at sea like Night like nothing but itself
vertical recall depth-surface slippage weight
some blue likely to run over chase down moon
stalk of blindness suited in
horrible chair dictaphone spectacles
beginning of nothing, withering into white
headless worm, cones rods, older than fish,
silver: unpublished novel too small to read

XIX

knock on wood Berlin summer 1892 attempted
photograph the soul storm in the archipelago
clouds ambitious of becoming water petitions
clothe the woman across the table taps his tank
repines Formica daily tabloid crossword marriage
metal in our gut sings, Mike, we detonate windows
it doesn't help the bus if you step into traffic
how close you have to come to register zero

XX

returned to chalk floating lights in car park
rolled from bed to tethered mother moon
departs traindoor drawn into bowed pain
discharge shines on curved section of nailed egg
processed slacks bluff against understated
memories compete for space at night you twitch
partdead Apolyon's candle blown, my holed
tongue swallows: best black, horse-bread

XXI

by Sarah collecting walnuts to harvest ink
lens eyebrow carved in suet
you'll never be released she improvises
call soul the odour of this windowless
chamber expecting prick of rosewater
core temperature experimental procedures split
twin the form of the bone is really similar
bone of Luz excuses a lifetime's fruitless search

XXII

fullrack wire-music waters can bullet
gravity of address travel business class
hireling peasant throws up arms
what is staged is also bought at price
from hyacinth garden when the Iraq war
started I'm a Californian & go outside
paint cactus trophy somebody records
what I say publishes that banality
impact beef stops mimicry: a true fall

XXIII

modernist architects rounded specs
ink dull-eye stack all sharpness
straight torture police in buttoned uniforms
german green make the place seem gay
he reported not many Jews found
we saw Warsaw burn & Modlin being burnt
stirring spectacle inherited wealth liver
spots Houston oilmen: no atonement, none

XXIV

educated at Edinburgh & in Holland ordained
minister of Athelstaneford he published in
1747 The Grave a didactic poem of the starred
graveyard school consisting of some 800 lines
blank verse celebrates horrors of death
fractured soul or skate cold dish of Blake
pilgrim clawing through walls of clay
tenement madness by empty mouth possessed

XXV

dollar-bulk captures Mafia weather, Sicilian-American
Balkan Ukrainian Siberian Jew
long-coats all of a piece on pier
we will sink your laughter-curated cow talk
cows they know & the rituals of steppe death
necklace light fellates black shoe – 'who's
paying?' – & carefully they step ashore, craft
heads out to redundant statuary, sunken fleet

XXVI

let out hooks & eyes if dressing required
simulate slack love text one thing
image quite another, what's done lends
lion-winged boat a constant glare
who commissioned story pass across coffee
table in Switzerland, barber in latex
bodysuit shot 3 times, midway no way
sleep leaks & garbage is the final reason

AFTERMATH

Thus does the 'Necessary Angel' of the poetic arrive to save the 'Angel of History' from dying of melancholy in a suffocating world of ruins.
Youssef Ishaghpour

To narrow the subject down to the question of poetics, Taussig rules out the idea (put forward by Lévi-Strauss, among others) that the shaman's song amounts to an ordering of internal chaos, for the song itself is unintelligible, 'part of a baroque mosaic of discourses woven through stories, jokes, interjections, and hummings taking place not only through and on top of one another during the actual seance but after it as well.'
Anthony Mellors

My favourite politician was Arizona Senator Barry Goldwater, who reminded me of Tom Mix, and there wasn't any way to explain that to anybody.
Bob Dylan

PATRICK HAMILTON

PATRICK HAMILTON IN ST LEONARDS ON SEA

'The sea! The sea! What of the sea?
The sea!
The solution – salvation! The sea! Why not?'
Patrick Hamilton

a bone, a Norman bone
scavenged from pitted shelf, rain
early, against delight of snow, failed roads
meat as it's fired, citadel stagnant with peace
hung in harness, brother spirits, late whisky
from pharmacist, a gentleman commoner
tyre track distinguishing narrow skull
Pat, Paddy, powers to your elbow
marine parenthesis, bed above butcher's slab
harnessed in bracers, shirtless, blindlight
smell and texture of chartered streets
you step fastidious into the young girl's body
her shame, geyser bath, soapflakes
sticky in tight hair, like flying
old values, old men: cigarette breakfast

II

Karl Marx & Hopalong Cassidy: this time apparently
you can trust the black shirt rider, saddlebum
smarter than singing cowboy, white-hat Roy
as beard, secular Jewish patriarch
granite paperweight holding down Highgate
it's confusing, headline backwards
canted road hidden from promenade,
wake up last night's radio, shadow of invasion
sea hiccups, every wave a dog's head,
cork waistcoat, cork room, memory used up
'that's you done to a nice turn, sir'
hands tremble, three air shots on a 9-holer
game's over, no more commuter trains
files thicken, print faints
the thin book it'll cost you fifty notes

if you agree to oppose, you agree
Hamilton never got his head around Marxism
confused coarse golf with horizonless steppes
tanks 'roll' into Bluewater, confirm television
threat, when the car crunched Earl's Court
his brother, fellow Norman, was in Victoria
watching the Marx Brothers in 'The Cocoanuts'
Freddie Mills borrowed a fairground rifle
to shoot himself, suspect vehicle, exploitation
of complimentary parking space up west
pass me the knout & the knot tightens
roped cabin trunk transports body parts
uneconomic migrants
try 'Hamilton's Drop' watered whisky
pissed into the hold of container ships

IV

gun-product collage, poetic 'objects' of mass observers
armpits eyebrows private life of midwives
sheer bollocks said H turning from rattle
slatted blinds concrete & pleasure
warden cadging light from cab driver
no hot water to scour dental plate
Naafi-style cafeteria breakfast Gielgud
holding free hand like a slack prick
I want war, H, to end it:
Yale lock, the difficulty in dying
To Save A Life! Do not interfere with this equipment

V

Mexican Fast Food from 5 to 11, Urban
Conflict Simulation Internet Access
if I had a gun I could kill myself cleanly
leave others to write up the mess
easier to swallow than a No.9 iron he said
everything tastes like marmalade
a ghost play without ghosts
plains of marzipan moving sand
the Egyptians I understand watch the same
sunrise it only takes about three years

caught Hamilton's tail squeezed juice
peardrops dissolving in milk
when he touched fingers to temple he bled
hair fell in marmalade, wife's
a toff, sickbed, autographed bat
imprint of her buttocks, moving south
& stopping is a curse, karma of
unbricked villa. The earlier applicant
suggested movies in an upstairs room, Lang
Hitchcock, dancing girls, projector beam
cone of blue smoke: that trick
they went for the usual crusty hotpot
too close, too loud,
20,000 streets under the sea, nothing
in the can to touch Max Von Sydow
splaying cold fingers, raising stiff arm
disbelief, a blister in her palm

refusing to read or even read about Billy Budd
climbed Melville not yet born
seaboots & long-coat in glycerine soft
ascent driven starwards mizzen-mast
'a great writer but unreadable'
bit above himself lost in computer pool
spoke Scotch & travelled once to America
20,000 spectators looking from blue yonder
dissolute faces red-paint fire
man he knew should possess grain & water
so give himself up to his judges & swing
avoiding gibbet gibbeted at dock gates
bone pendulum, pulp writer's winter fever

why does Stacey from Holiday Rewards have to be late
Americana, beamed from sub-continent
to swing & mimic, allowed to go so far before
I say no with mock serious conviction
or, better, 'Go away'. He dig it, the German
cleared by truth commission repentance
private resolution, disturbed by glow under pier
Hamilton couldn't tell left from right,
Hitler Youth costume in wardrobe,
no aberration against disorganisation
of hot places where older Bavarian gentlemen
hide out: to be here, to be fixed
in the matter-toffee of narrative
mouse on sticky pad
death by screwdriver, how they scuttle
legless, behind fridge
according to whim: in darkness or light

AFTERMATH

Three years slumber on the banks of the Ocean.
William Blake

It explained his dreams. The Chinese caused his dreams. Every terror
and queerness of sleep, even unspeakability – it is painted in China white.
Don DeLillo

Pistol Pete hadn't played professionally for a while, and he was thought
of as forgotten. I hadn't forgotten about him, though. Some people seem
to fade away but when they are truly gone, it's like they didn't fade away
at all.

Bob Dylan

THE OPENING OF THE FIFTH SEAL:
WALTER SICKERT, ALEISTER CROWLEY
& THE CHAPMAN BROTHERS

BURIED AT SEA

'None of them knew the colour of the sky'
Stephen Crane

it doesn't take long to drown
she said
women more than men can't run
long clothes drag them down
two waves she said
a few hundred yards from town
money is deep it doesn't reach
under stone the sand is pure
a man throws the sea back
another moves against the current
buzzing for ring pulls, foreign coins
ringing the seasons never stops

Light abdicates, pulls back, as we witness it. Days at the seaside find resolution this way. The slender mother, down there, watches over her novel child, his back to the waves. You'll notice a distinct line where newly-exposed sand meets steep shingle. He slithers, the boy, scrambles on the insecure slope. The mother selects the stones he throws, never reaching an incoming tide. The older father, at the crest of the ridge, is in easy conversation with another woman, a friend. The child's animation, his repeated actions, are the focus of all our attention. We remember previous children, earlier selves.

Vernal Equinox. There have been no bombs, recently, in London.

My back fits comfortably against the seawall. This is a familiar, solitary place: the experience of sitting with the weight of newspaper, brushing off sand after a morning swim. Friends, families, strangers — even Metropolitan Hasids, saffron-robed Buddhists — are forced to improvise, toy with future memories, to postpone the taking of decisions. The English Channel is a good excuse, meal over, for giving shape to a shapeless day. Potatoes, mayonnaise. Cold meats. The disparate group reconvenes. There is a car to be claimed, the return. We acknowledge our unexpressed satisfaction, our slight regret, that it is over, the instant of society.

Two young women, one with notable red hair, walk with purpose down the left margin of the beach. They know exactly what they are doing, in a place, it is obvious, they have never previously visited. And will not see again: this day, this time. The sharpness of the evening, gulls waiting to reclaim their rocks. The original beach has been divided into sections of about ninety yards by groynes, staked wooden barriers; a sequence of stone gardens, marine allotments. Dog-people, fisherman, eccentric swimmers: they have their preferred zones. Some carry trowels and plastic bags. Others encourage their animals by throwing balls or sticks into the sea. They are out at first light, or before, with the couples who stretch and breathe. Beach sleepers. The mad ones who sit, following pedestrians with hungry eyes, waiting for the chance to speak.

Where to look? How to manage this thing, gracefully? The taller girl, with the hair — Polish, Russian — strips, briskly, to her underwear.

Or it might be a swimming costume, black. She marches into the sea. Her shorter, sturdier friend is completely naked. She stands in the local surf, which is rolling, tumbling. First stars. Warning light flashing on the Royal Soverign. The tall one plunges, strikes out, a few strokes and she turns, stands waiting, loses her footage, comes ashore.

They dress, not bothering to rub themselves down. They don't talk. No rucksacks, no carrier bags. They pass us, side by side, up the ramp, away west along the promenade, in the direction of Bulverhythe.

After this event, more remote, more implicated than cinema, other twilight figures come together; smiling, they discuss what they have seen. If, in fact, it was the same thing. And how this place adapts so well to its varied uses.

STANDING MAN IN SPECTACLES, LECTURING SEATED WOMEN

in the glue factory of the eye
theorists argue a strap
secure a bulging leather case
head of the victim
gardenia in hair, flowering exhibit

MEAT RAFFLE

Brook came down to consult the Beast
travelling to the wrong place
in search of Faustian magic
heroin
fatal contract
Oxford return, world triumph
London Cannibal Killer First Picture

Sickert imported Dieppe fishwife, burnt orange snatch, brave Madame
talking of arse-coughs, he posed blade's
length of trouser just so, inward gaze
fucking cheap but nobody to talk at
the cast of Proust's novel primitive
cinematograph, outer harbour
who will he kiss in Venice
'Kilburn-in-the-Sea', 3 in boat
engorged, six-year-old child, darkwater
lightens the palette, falsely
accused, black toast, scabs peel
pushes mother back into frame
slash canvas loses skin, further
exile not available on temporary basis
I find comfort in familiar brands
put bear through the gate, green
hands fat with bottled leaves

NIGHT VISITOR

Tongue nestled between mildewed patches
on the steep plate, soaking up sauce
taking a little brown into pink, was
Crowley's own, the Night Visitor he said
withdrawing leaving guests to fend
for themselves, sick headache
while he fished for a vein tapping the hypo
like Victor's raw-edged cock
hot stuff didn't sting the Ridge
ash in throat, landfill graves
a bad smell, sweet roses sold
in forecourts, petrol gets in your pores
and young ladies apply to draw the caul
from red eyes, bald as winter
I am more real wrote the dame
losing her marbles, swimming naked down
deleted roads, talking back to French gulls

FISHY OILS

'A book must be the axe for a frozen sea inside us'
Franz Kafka

Don't deal he said in mystifications
demons conspiracies vampirism
an old & honoured tradition once you acquire
a taste for blood, let me have it straight
around the houses, boy, paint the sea
under a green canopy of urban jungle
the BP longhouse peddles cargo trash
cruisers & Balkan migrants, vendor
prays to monitor screen, vivid drama
the consolations of elsewhere
in colour: Crowley used spit for (baby) oil

Halliburton remarried Elizabeth Taylor fed her
generously on petroleum jelly, by spoon, plastered
billboard giganticism of road to airport
James Dean dances, Brando does business
bamboo water-scoop fishing shack
operated by secretly dispersed
Chinese labourers (on starvation wages)
'what is that – fish?'
'something dead?'
spit cloak slack bulk
marine western tarnished angel
earthed by Ben Johnson who rode like
the horse was on top of him & later in getaway
played Enron fixer petrochemical baron
sandstorms across the border
dawn-waves flop all day
cod sacrifice lives to ward off bird flu

MODERATO CANTABILE

Who is that dark thing behind shaded woman
caught in beam, exposed arm
forearmed fate, lifeforce spent, exhaustion
of fountains day-for-night radiance
fool's gold better than none, sure
of temporary status, rewind to red
or crow: angle of vorticist collar
nurselike conviction private wounds
high clamp the label, guileless
removal of other wedding band, video bay
unbutton'd wet-
lipped, the shocking scale of
waste operatives, layered
in lash, it would seem desirable, absolutely so
blaze of whiteness in formal
nude, wherefore doth he weep
sag folds racially august
mongrel intelligence, double plot
servant & pre-spoiled priest, their candle

MONEY MYSTICS

oaf Benedict, razored Ulsterman, brain & mouth
they sat the Frenchman serial abuser
in the Elland Road pit filing nail bombs, later
black vest, loose suit, sockless for convict wedding
actors are holes in the frame, harbour smoke
maritime heritage, groom tagged
& branded, manacles out of shot, thin Italy
political place less so than Shakespeare's new
imaging, cinema lies most when it exploits the truth

BROKEN HAT

ee cummings : poetry endorsed by movie stars
Marilyn Monroe, lips moving,
new tall bridegroom, waits on smile (wolfish)
Rod Steiger (blink) weeps for chat show
cummings article of faith
it is saturday afternoon on the welsh bay
light (6 floors up) lifts a little after rain
Sunday says wristwatch
we have to go with that, out into Europe

SICKERT AT DIEPPE

'just like a watering can, the shape'

      overnight, an island
      low-black,
      grounddown teeth
      imagined as icicles

Churchill's mother-in-law's armchair
drawn out to harbour, he couldn't
serve or service the daughter, compromised
fishwife, Mme Villain
city halls & churches cleared for returnees,
mutilés de guerre, future beggars

painter in wrong town hears war
new sharp art without
trusted method of preparation
no poem but anecdote, postcoital
lunch at convenient café, he dined
at home, went anywhere with noise,
handled workers like workers
the favour of art, artlessly spread
tide changes, we manoeuvre and fail

'nature in the wind, and nature in the vision of men'

he has landed it is finished 30 yards out
tartan rug roadside
picnic in wilting sun, the reservoir
Walter Scott tower its mechanical
ripples, brown froth stink of ammonia
in the underpass as drinkers congregate
solitaries accepted without hesitation
sodality of shoreline, alcoves
polyphonic babble
atonement, spitwash, bracing bacterium
from the far side Sickert watches a lesser
painter walk unharmed beneath the waves,
lesson scorned: I wait, slow
tunnel, electrified train, girl in red dress
another body in the local woods

CASTLED

In cold mist, so he tells it, winter, the top of the building. A script (horror, autobiography), he's been working with, on and off, for most of his adult life. No longer a viable project, the career. Screaming Jaguars jump the kerb of industrial estates, bent cops with slack ties: the same pitch sold a dozen times. Revenge. Hard time. Unfaithful wife. Lost loot. The same faces in the brown envelope: wife, wives, houses, fame. All gone. He keeps the Sky screen, the kind you dread in hard-drinking Bull Ring saloons (the provenance). Paperback books are horizontally stacked. He still writes in the old way; wine, spliff, full ashtray. Fish-eye lens in thick door. He never responds to the entry-phone.

The figure outside, on the terrace, is dead. Hair like Howard Hughes. Marine Court: an ice-age Vegas. He is unclothed, spiked with needles. Crack house raiders, ecstasy casuals bored with cars, they haunt the decks of this ruin. Feet in foil trays. Everything smells of posthumous curry.

The writer shouts. His breath an empty speech bubble. Slides the glass door, shouts in the zombie's face. The thing he has invented, his plot, is coming apart. Loose pyjama trousers on visible pelvis. The poor man is punctured with needles and tubes. Muttering numbers, holding a hand to protect his face, he disappears.

Cancer patient, it is later revealed. Terminal. Confused. The wrong floor, simply that, morphine reverie. Sleepwalking the bounds, Elsinore. Nothing to impart. This fatherless man, the writer, is shamed. Absolutely. Now he has a story to offer.

HASTINGS OPERA

In film they step out of the opera
strip originates movie house consequence
a mugging of the innocent, bite that little
silver bullet & suffer a culture free
evacuation, waft of interior sound unheard
on darkening promenade, all society attends
reluctant manageress & lovely daughter
failing bookshop man, solo in bar, late
convalescents, halt & lame in privileged
tilt at surtitles, Traviata
Ukraine travellers punt spic
warble, high notes held, stunted lead
on platform heels, most of the dignitaries
disguised in chorus line,
consumption a fissure in the rock
bonfire party on prom, glory
of place without memory
efflorescence of pulled, smudged colour
blue sandals and a door marked CHURCH

VOLAVERUNT

'Goya, presumably, will always work late on a Friday'
Simon Bates

she had to use lined paper
he could not live away from the sea
(tried Yorkshire woke up sweating)
keeps a bookshop rises at five
window open, the glare, fan going
one true sentence and take it from there
eyes failing, few books, procures morphine
some of his teeth fell out, the quality
of truth was not an absolute
like green, it was shifty like
turquoise, neither word nor colour
really works, you iron my sentences
the plains are not ocean, magic
mushrooms will soon be illegitimate
long life passed in an instant
he was out for hours & stayed within
his depth, silver paper wards off
gulls better than shop-bought owl

26 AUGUST 1875

Cpt. Webb, an hour out, swallowed
a swift half from his cousin's boat
porpoises appeared
drawn by heat of body-drench
followers shot, wounded, didn't kill
he took a saucer of beef tea
breaststroking into the swell,
18-20 strokes per minute,
the fret lifted
revealing Dover Cliff, facing
the wrong way,
in weary expectation of France

POST-OFFICE

The generosity of government assures
a 50pc concession on the television licence
on production of an original certificate
confirming status, that you are,
authentically and irredeemably, blind

The film-maker Andrew Kötting makes little distinction between two words, exercise and exorcise. Where there is a problem in life or art, family, health, contingent worlds, he plunges, leaps, lifts; or sets off around the ragged fringes of Britain in a camper van, carrying with him his perky grandmother, Gladys, and his daughter, Eden. Who suffers from Joubert's Syndrome. And who, as a young voyager, talked in sign language and trilled like a wise bird. The film of this stuttering, mock-heroic odyssey was completed in 1996 and was called *Gallivant*. It made Britain a better place to live, drawing as it did on random elegies of citizens mired, for better or worse, in their localities. Here was a frenetic excursionism, the singular day out that goes on for ever. A brave confrontation of the immense and incorruptible fact of the sea.

Another time, dealing with an inconvenient death or looming trauma, Kötting slipped in, without authorisation, among the runners at the start of the London Marathon. He was grabbed, by security men, a few yards short of the finish; never receiving his silver cape and complimentary Mars bar. Memories of a difficult and abusive father were countered by dragging an inflatable version of the grinning dad around the world, from Hastings to Mexico. The Day of the Dead and a flowery grave.

And so I found myself in an East Sussex sea-front car park at 1.30am, wondering which of the suspect vehicles might hold the Kötting brothers and their associates, a genial and extended, Mafia-lite family. Ten years had passed since the completion of *Gallivant*, hard times in which a Kötting feature, *This Filthy Earth*, had appeared and disappeared - and funding proposals swallowed many long and tedious months. Let it all go then: in a cross-channel swim. The whole mob, three brothers, a brother-in-law, the actor Xavier Tchilli (from *This Filthy Earth*) and Sean Lock, Kötting scriptwriter and stand-up comedian, would swim as a relay, one hour at a stretch. Sean wouldn't be standing up for long.

It sounded very reasonable, in the pub. They even floated the notion of touching shore and swimming straight back. From the safety of a seventh-floor balcony, I'd watched Andrew plough through the briny, like Johnny Weissmuller or Lex Barker, from the direction of Bexhill down to Hastings Pier. But this was a safe marine set in which to play Tarzan, among buoyant turds and sneering gulls. Air-Sea Rescue had been called out, once or twice, alerted to a potential suicide attempt by loungers on the esplanade. But the open-sea business was a sterner test. Overshadowed, as it was, by the spectre of David Walliams. If the smooth celebrity could knock off this nautical marathon so effortlessly, where was the necessary anguish, the torment, the existential screech?

The support vessel was pitching gently against the marina, in the charge of its less supportive captain, Michael Oram. A Ricky Tomlinson lookalike who did a very good line in deflating the hubris of enthusiastic amateurs. 'Give it up now, lads. The pubs open early down here.' The vessel had been booked because it had the right name, *Gallivant*. Swimmers and sailors are loud with superstition. The Kötting associates, on the dock, fizzed with macho banter, but already there was dread in their eyes, a dryness in the mouth. One of the camera crew gulped down a thermos of leak and potato soup, in the well founded belief that when the mess spewed out on the deck it would look exactly the same as it had going in. A single yellow bucket was provided to cope with the liquid contributions of six swimmers, two film-makers, three crew members and your reporter. Whose only qualification, really, was a strong stomach and the willingness to fetch and carry towels and energy supplements, to bear witness to the worst the sea could offer. (A strong conviction that Géricault's *Raft of the 'Medusa'* was a proper role model.) No life-jackets were provided. Food and drink would not be required.

Captain Oram scratched his belly and took the readings. 'It's what we call whacky weather, a hardened swimmer's day.' Wind on the turn, gusting from 4 to 5, white caps frisking outside the harbour. He agreed, reluctantly, on a trial hour, which would be swum by Andrew, as team leader and senior citizen. To give this madness the right metaphor, Kötting begun by pissing a starting line across the beach below Shakespeare's Cliff. Echoes of *Lear*. 'The fishermen that walk upon the beach/ Appear like mice, and yond tall anchoring bark/ Diminish'd to her cock...' There is indeed much talk of diminished cocks, much plucking and chaffing, as relay swimmers haul themselves out of the water, grooming salt-sticky pubic clumps. 'I haven't seen myself this size,' said Sean Lock, 'since I was seven-years-old.'

His hour done, Kötting fights for breath. 'It feels like the boat is doing weird things. It's going at the wrong angle and you're just hanging on.' The night is close and dark; Kötting, out there, no more than a green jelly-fish luminescence, the glow of his attached lightstick.

'If you're the strongest swimmer,' said Oram, 'we'll pack it in now. You're looking at twenty-odd hours.' The second man, Xavier, was struggling. 'He's been in five minutes and he hasn't moved. He's doing breaststroke.' But Kötting is resolute. 'If it takes twenty hours, it takes twenty hours. Whatever happens, we're going to stick with it.'

What happens is: a drunken support vessel struggling to hold game novices, who fight the swell, swallowing copious drafts of channel. Some retch out there, coughing tragically like clubbed seals. And some wait until they're dragged back on deck. Where they lie in heaps, grey-green and clammy as reversed wet suits. I note and appreciate discriminations of vomit. The film crew gave themselves up long before we lost sight of land. Brother Mark lurched to the stern and did his best not to fill the hanging dinghy. 'After he's brought up the bile,' the captain smirked, 'it'll be coffee dregs. Then the lining of his stomach.' To say nothing of a white froth, like ectoplasm, or chewed soap. Food traces of meals taken decades ago in a country they may never see again.

Wind and tide carry our swimmers forward. Brother-in-law Ian, who has a damaged Achilles tendon, picks up the pace. Mark Kötting, half-dead on board, hurtles through the sea, with long powerful strokes. They discover the truth of what the captain told them: 'You're better in the water.' Astonishingly, the team perform more efficiently on the second leg. And then the third.

Long after the cliffs of Dover have been lost, and before there is even a mirage of France, the boat that set off alongside us passes on the way home. Professionals known as 'The Nancy Boys', they've knocked it off in eight and a bit hours. 'Doesn't count,' says Kötting, 'they're Australian.' His youngest brother, Joey, back from California, is trying not to choke on his Russian unorthodox beard, as he fights to hold close to the boat, avoiding diesel fumes.

It's a close run thing, sun sinking, rocks of Cap Gris-Nez, tide on the turn, but they do it. Ian touches France, after Andrew and Xavier have gone into the sea for the third time. It's heroic and inspiring, this foolishness. How they support one another and carry through a fantasy for which there can be no preparation. Fourteen hours and seventeen minutes is a useful time. Their lives contracted to a willed intensity, stomachs voided, nerves stretched. Imprinted images that will never fade. A French gull, offering promise of land, touches Joey's shoulder and stays with him, peddling against the waves. Offering a confirming mime about the difficulty of transferring out of your natural medium, from land or from air, into this sweet and sticky soup.

PLATZ ANGST

Sentiment cooks nicely in window fall
Paris a very traditional place to come to die,
or rehearse, or lose a slice of foot
you can't write Luxembourg gardens set
words in right order, listening
to Cambodian speech, it crosses
the weave, bad things
river tunnels, immigrant hymns
formless misery the stairs he runs skips
into reversed sound, small projectiles
never sees, the big mistake, parsing
song in chalk bricolage,
months are mince, VAT return music
dripping rain, black streets,
I'm still a million miles from you

...to place where pen writes number
inscribes date on cheque signature
seals adhesive white rectangle
the number on yellow
buoy, lovely because contaminated
live fecal matter growing on laminate
cancelled place where kids stand
hinterland of potential, people
literally taking pleasure meadow
coarse intention, although
back of it are garages, stacked studios
They come to shore for Chelsea harbours
wicked boys, cut motors
road a false note, equinoctial heat
we simmer & boil, hands in murky
water, fins: our boat is blue, it passes

pearlgrey suede swerves barges aside
red error, hair armour accessories
attendant cologne blue-silk truss
the trashed Caprichos, mickey mousetrap
'thirteen and a half - plus VAT'
hymenal hygiene of white box,
we're inside the inside
'they've taken children's classics & reworked
horror war, the human condition'
Euro-optimism built on dredged sand
looking at art is the art
worm tentacles, tactical kisses
no front line it happens everywhere

9 OCTOBER 2005

I climb from cooling sea
to sit on low concrete shelf
'You'll live forever,' the woman says
'but why, darling, why?'

AFTERMATH

Everything is here. Baptismal records, report cards, postcards, divorce petitions, canceled checks, daily timesheets, tax returns, property lists, postoperative x-rays, photos of knotted string, thousands of pages of testimony, of voices droning in hearing rooms in old courthouse buildings, an incredible haul of human utterance. It lies so flat on the page, hangs so still in the lazy air, lost to syntax and other arrangement, that it resembles a kind of mind-spatter, a poetry of lives muddied and dripping in language.

Don DeLillo

Already he did not look like himself any more, his grimacing expression that of a complete stranger, expressing like a chinaman, some quite strange and unrecognizable emotion.

Iris Murdoch

ACKNOWLEDGEMENTS

Some of these poems, or earlier versions of them, were published here and there, in ephemeral magazines and deleted web-sites. I thank all those responsible, even as I fail to do them the courtesy of remembering their titles and occasions.

Twelve of the texts from 'Marinade' were handset, as an artist's book, by Susanna Edwards. And offered, as an edition of seven copies, in a boxed set: *Marinade XII*. I'd like to express my gratitude to Susanna for the care she took in working with my images, snapshots, newspaper cuttings, book covers, to produce the thing I was barely capable of describing.

SELECT VIEWING

Michelangelo Antonioni. *The Passenger* (1975).
Ingmar Bergman. *Persona* (1966).
    Hour of the Wolf (1967).
    The Shame (1968).
    The Passion of Anna (1969).
John Boutling. *Brighton Rock* (1947).
John Brahm. *Hangover Square* (1945).
Marlon Brando. *One-Eyed Jacks* (1961).
Peter Brook. *Moderato Cantabile* (1960).
William Castle. *Shanks* (1974).
Francis Ford Coppola. *Apocalypse Now* (1979).
David Cronenberg. *Crash* (1996).
Abel Ferrara. *The Addiction* (1994)
Mike Figgis. *Leaving Las Vegas* (1995)
Robert Florey, Joseph Stanley. *The Cocoanuts* (1929).
John Ford. *The Grapes of Wrath* (1940).
Sam Fuller. *Pickup on South Street* (1953).
Jean-Luc Godard. *Le Mépris* (1963).
    Pierrot le fou (1965).
    Made in USA (1966).
    Détective (1984)
    Allemagne 90 année neuf zéro (1991).
Alfred Hitchcock. *Rope* (1948).
    Psycho (1960).
John Huston. *The Red Badge of Courage* (1951).
    The Misfits (1960).
Alejandro Gonzalez Inarritu. *21 Grams* (2003).
Elia Kazan. *On the Waterfront* (1954).
    A Face in the Crowd (1955).
    East of Eden (1955).
Irving Kershner. *Stakeout on Dope Street* (1958).
Henry King. *Tender is the Night* (1962).
Andrew Kötting. *Gallivant* (1996).
Fritz Lang. *Dr Mabuse, der Spieler* (1922).
    The Thousand Eyes of Dr Mabuse (1961).

Joshua Logan. *Bus Stop* (1956).
Joseph Losey. *The Damned* (1962).
Sidney Lumet. *A View from the Bridge* (1961).
David Lynch. *Mulholland Dr.* (2001)
Andrzej Munk. *Passenger* (1963).
F.W. Murnau. *Nosferatu* (1922).
               Sunrise (1927).
Newsreel archive: The House Committee on Un-American Activities.
François Ozon. *The Swimming Pool* (2003).
Sam Peckinpah. *The Getaway* (1972).
Chris Petit. *Negative Space* (1999).
Otto Preminger. *Bonjour Tristesse* (1957).
Nicholas Ray. *The Lusty Men* (1952).
Roberto Rossellini. *Germany Year Zero* (1948).
               Viaggio in Italia (1954).
Don Sharp. *The Face of Fu Manchu* (1965).
Dr Henry Sinclair. 16mm home movies (1943-50).
Douglas Sirk. *Written on the Wind* (1956).
               The Tarnished Angels (1957).
George Stevens. *Giant* (1956).
François Truffaut. *Day for Night* (1973).
               The Green Room (1978).
Roger Vadim. *Et Dieu Créa la Femme* (1956).
               Blood and Roses (1960).
Luchino Visconti. *The Damned* (1969).
Andy Warhol. *Chelsea Girls* (1967)
David Wickes. *Sweeney!* (1976).

AN INSTRUMENT
FOR THE IMPEACHMENT
OF DEAD CINEMAS

Worple Press is an independent publishing house that specialises in poetry, art and alternative titles.

Worple Press can be contacted at:
PO Box 328, Tonbridge, Kent TN9 1WR Tel 01732 368 958
email: theworpleco@aol.com.

Trade orders: Central Books, 99 Wallis Road, London E9 5LN
Tel 0845 4589911

TITLES INCLUDE:

The Verbals **– Kevin Jackson in Conversation with Iain Sinclair** (A5 Price £12.00 / 20 Euros ISBN 0-9530947-9-0, pp. 148)

'Highly interesting.' *The Guardian*
'Cultists will be eager to get their hands on it.' *TLS*
'Worple Press have done it again... this sparkling introduction to Sinclair and his world.'   *The Use of English*

Against Gravity **– Beverley Brie Brahic**
(A5 Price £8.00 ISBN 1-905208-03-0, pp 72)

Full Stretch **– Anthony Wilson**
(Price £8 /10 Euros ISBN 1-905208-04-9, pp 104)

Sailing to Hokkaido **– Joseph Woods**
(A5 Price £6.00 ISBN 0 9530947-6-6, pp 60)

Bearings **– Joseph Woods**
(A5 Price £8.00 / 10 Euros ISBN 1905208-00-6, pp 64)

A Ruskin Alphabet - **Kevin Jackson**
(A6 Price £4.50 ISBN 0 9530947-2-3, pp. 88)
'you may like to consult *A Ruskin Alphabet* by Kevin Jackson, a collection of facts and opinions on ruskin and Ruskinites, together with a variety of pithy remarks from the man himself'   *TLS*

Looking In All Directions – **Peter Kane Dufault**
(A5 Price £10.00 ISBN 0 9530947-5-8, pp. 188)

'Wonderful stuff'   *Ted Hughes*

The Great Friend and Other Translated Poems – **Peter Robinson**
(A5 Price £8.00 ISBN 0-9530947-7-4, pp. 75)
Poetry Book Society Recommended Translation

Stigmata – **Clive Wilmer**
(A5 Price £10.00 / 15 Euros ISBN 1-905208-01-4, pp. 28)

'a brilliant piece of work which brings honour to our time'
Sebastian Barker

FORTHCOMING TITLES

Bowl — **Elizabeth Cook**

To be In the Same World — **Peter Kane Dufault**

Warp and Weft — **an anthology of Worple writing**